THE HOW AND WHY WONDER BOOK OF
FLIGHT

Written by HAROLD JOSEPH HIGHLAND, B.S., M.S., Ph.D.
Associate Professor, College of Business Administration,
Long Island University

Illustrated by GEORGE J. ZAFFO

Editorial Production: DONALD D. WOLF

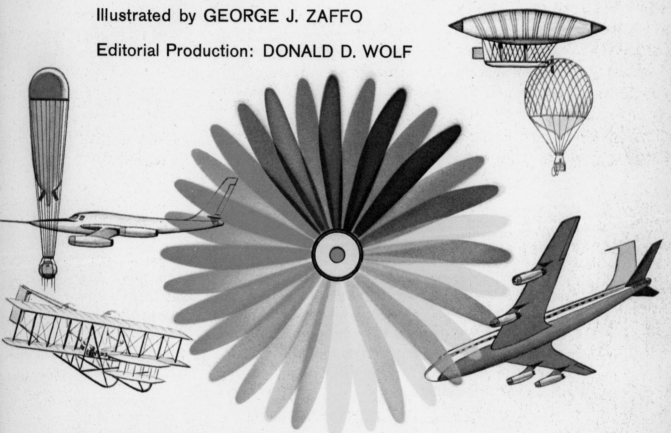

Edited under the supervision of
Dr. Paul E. Blackwood.
Washington, D. C.

Text and illustrations approved by
Oakes A. White, Brooklyn Children's Museum, Brooklyn, New York

WONDER BOOKS • NEW YORK
A Division of GROSSET & DUNLAP, Inc.

Introduction

Scientists are filled with curiosity and this leads them to search for answers through exploration and experiment. This *How and Why Wonder Book* amply demonstrates how, over the years, the search for ways to move through the air has led to present-day miracles of flight. The book will help young scientists to widen their horizons of discovery about the unending efforts to conquer and explore space.

To fly like a bird has always been a hope of man. We know this from legend, mythology and recorded history. The hope has burned in man's dreams and challenged him to make the attempt. First it seemed like a dream of improbable fulfillment. Then gradually, from fumbling beginnings, success was achieved. Man flew! And now, in many ways, he flies better than the birds—higher and faster and beyond the air.

The How and Why Wonder Book of Flight helps the reader to relive the fascinating story of man's increasing mastery of the air from early attempts to present-day accomplishments. It takes the reader from the first flight of balloons, which merely drifted with the wind, to the amazing X-15 with its phenomenal speeds and man's orbiting of the earth in a spaceship. Here are answers to many questions about early types of planes, jets, missiles and rockets. Why does an airplane fly? What is the jet stream? How do pilots navigate in bad weather? And many others.

Every person who is excited about living in the space age, at a time when man continues his effort to explore the solar system and when scheduled flights may well carry passengers to the moon, should have this book of basic information about flight for reading and reference.

Paul E. Blackwood

Dr. Blackwood is a professional employee in the U. S. Office of Education. This book was edited by him in his private capacity and no official support or endorsement by the Office of Education is intended or should be inferred.

Contents

	Page
DREAMS OF FLIGHT	5
Who was the first man to fly?	6
What is ethereal air?	6
What is an ornithopter?	7
THE AGE OF AEROSTATICS	8
How did aerostatics help man to fly?	8
How did the first balloonists fly?	9
Why did the hydrogen balloon fly?	10
Who were other famous early balloonists?	10
How does a dirigible differ from a balloon?	11
When did the first dirigible fly?	11
What is a zeppelin?	11
Why did the zeppelin disappear?	14
THE AIR PIONEERS	14
Who is the father of aeronautics?	14
When did the first powered airplane fly?	15
How does a glider fly?	15
Who made the first successful powered flight?	16
How did early aviation progress?	17
How did airplanes "shrink" the world?	19
Who made the first nonstop solo flight across the Atlantic?	19
FAMOUS FIRSTS IN EARLY AVIATION	20
FLYING IN ANY DIRECTION	21
How did the helicopter originate?	21
How can you make a Cayley top?	21
Who were the early helicopter builders?	22
How does an autogyro fly?	22
Who perfected the helicopter?	23
How does the helicopter fly?	23
How do the modern ornithopters fly?	24
What is VTOL?	24
THEORY AND FACTS OF FLIGHT	25
Why does an airplane fly?	25
What makes an airplane go up and down?	26

	Page
How does an airplane turn?	26
How can you demonstrate *lift?*	27
How can you demonstrate the working of an elevator?	28
WHAT DO THE INSTRUMENTS TELL THE PILOT?	28
HIGHWAYS OF THE AIR	30
What are the airways?	31
Which plane has the right of way?	32
How do air markers help pilots to fly?	32
How do pilots fly in all types of weather?	32
FASTER THAN SOUND	33
When were jets first used?	34
How does a jet fly?	34
Ramjet and pulsejet	36
How a turbojet works	37
Why do they use turboprops?	38
What is the sound barrier?	38
How did the sound barrier change the shape of planes?	39
Why do planes fly in the jet stream?	39
What will future jet planes be like?	40
RECENT AVIATION HISTORY	41
ROCKETS, MISSILES AND SATELLITES	42
How were rockets first used?	42
Who were the rocket pioneers?	42
What makes a rocket fly?	43
What is a guided missile?	44
How do they guide missiles?	44
Why does a satellite stay up in the sky?	45
What do satellites *see* and *tell?*	46
STEPPINGSTONES INTO SPACE	47
Has man flown in a rocket?	47
What is Project Mercury?	48
What about the future?	48

Man gave the power of flight to gods and sacred animals. The winged bull is an Assyrian sculpture of the ninth century B.C.

The sphinx, a symbol of Egyptian royalty, wa[s] adopted by the Greeks. But it was given wings an[d] served as tomb sculpture in the sixth century B.C[.]

This detail from a Greek vase of the fourth century B.C. shows the mythical hero Bellerophon mounted on his winged horse Pegasus. Together, they slew the three-headed Chimera. Sculptures similar to these are exhibited at the Metropolitan Museum of Art, New York.

Dreams of Flight

The story of man's dream of flight, of his desire to reach the stars, is as old as mankind itself. It is easy to imagine that prehistoric man, faced with a fierce, attacking monster, yearned to spring up and fly away just like a bird.

In ancient folklore and religions, we have ample proof of this desire to fly. But desires and dreams cannot lift a man off the earth, and so the wondrous ability to fly was reserved for his gods. Each of the gods had some means of flight. In ancient Greece, Phaeton, son of Helios, the sun god, drove the wild horses that pulled the sun chariot. Mercury, the messenger of the gods, had a winged helmet and winged sandals. The

Out of man's ancient dream of flight came this extension of his desire — a winged lion (Middle Ages).

The woodcut by the German painter and engraver, Albrecht Dürer, depicts Daedalus and Icarus fleeing the island of Crete. But Icarus perished in the sea.

5

winged horse, Pegasus, was able to fly faster, farther and higher than any bird.

The dream of flight was universal. In ancient Egypt and Babylonia, they pictured winged bulls, winged lions and even men with wings. The ancient Chinese, Greeks, Aztecs of Central America, Iroquois of North America, all shared this dream.

According to Greek legend, Daedalus,

Who was the first man to fly?

the Athenian inventor, was the first man to fly. He and his son, Icarus, had been imprisoned on the island of Crete by King Minos. In order to escape, Daedalus shaped wings of wax into which he stuck bird feathers.

During their flight, Icarus flew too high and the sun melted the wax. He was drowned in the sea, and that body of water is still called the Icarian Sea in honor of the first man to lose his life in flying. The father is supposed to have continued his flight and reached Sicily, several hundred miles away.

There is also an English legend of King Bladud who, during his reign in the ninth century B.C., used wings to fly. But his flight was short-lived and he fell to his death.

A Frenchman named Besnier claimed that he flew the above contraption in the late seventeenth century.

The dream of flying continued, but in all the legends, the flier rose like a bird only to fall like a stone. It was more than twenty-six hundred years after King Bladud's flight that men flew up into the air and returned to earth safely.

The first man to approach flying on a

What is ethereal air?

scientific basis was Roger Bacon, an Englishman who lived during the thirteenth century. He envisioned the air about us as a sea, and he believed that a balloon could float on the air just as a boat did on water. His balloon, or air boat, was to be filled with *ethereal air* so that it might float on the air sea. We do not know what Bacon meant by ethereal air; yet, many still credit him with the basic concept of balloon flight.

Almost four hundred years later, Francesco de Lana, an Italian priest, applied Bacon's principle of air flight. He designed a boat, complete with mast

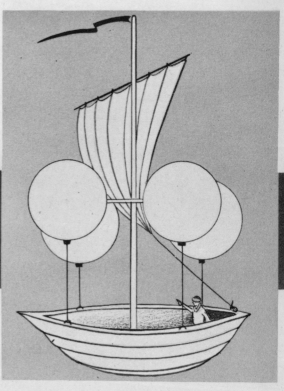

De Lana's air boat was held aloft by four spheres.

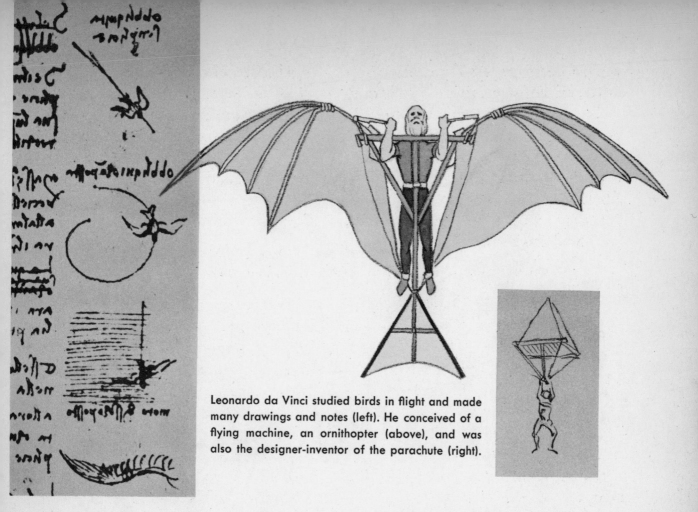

Leonardo da Vinci studied birds in flight and made many drawings and notes (left). He conceived of a flying machine, an ornithopter (above), and was also the designer-inventor of the parachute (right).

and sail, which would be held in the air by four hollow spheres. Each of the four balls was to be 20 feet in diameter and made of very thin copper. The air was to be removed from the balls so that they could float in the sky and lift the boat into the air.

De Lana's boat was never built since it was not possible to make spheres of such thin metal and such size in those days. Even if they had been built, the thin spheres would have been crushed by the pressure of the atmosphere.

Leonardo da Vinci was not only the greatest mathematician of the fifteenth century, but also a noted painter, architect, sculptor, engineer and musician. After studying the flight of birds and the movement of the air,

What is an ornithopter?

he reasoned that birds flew because they flapped their wings and that it was possible for man to do the same. Da Vinci designed the *ornithopter* (or-ni-THOP-ter), a flapping-wing flying machine. The wings were to be moved by a man's arms and legs.

Ornithopters were tried by many men. Robert Hooke experimented with this means of flight in England about 1650. He claimed he succeeded in flying, but he also wrote of his great difficulties to remain in the air. He is the first man who recognized that feathers were not needed for flight.

Many men tried and failed to fly with the ornithopter. It was not until 1890 that Octave Chanute discovered why this method would never succeed — man could not develop sufficient power with only his arms and legs.

7

The first balloon flights were made in 1783 when the Montgolfier brothers used heated air to make an ornate balloon rise.

One of the memorable early balloon flights was made by J. A. C. Charles, a French physicist, and one of the Robert brothers. The flight lasted over two hours, reaching a two-mile height.

The Age of Aerostatics

How did aerostatics help man to fly?

In 1643, Evangelista Torricelli demonstrated that the earth's atmosphere is more than just empty space. With his barometer, he proved that the atmosphere has weight and density, just like any gas. This discovery was the beginning of the science of *aerostatics*. Aerostatics (aero-STAT-ics) is the study of how an object is supported in the air by buoyancy; that is, its ability to float in air as a boat floats on water.

A milestone in this new science was reached ten years before the Declaration of Independence. Henry Cavendish, an English scientist, mixed iron, tin and zinc shavings with oil of vitriol and discovered a new gas which was lighter than air. Cavendish's "inflammable air" was later named "hydrogen" by the French chemist, Lavoisier.

8

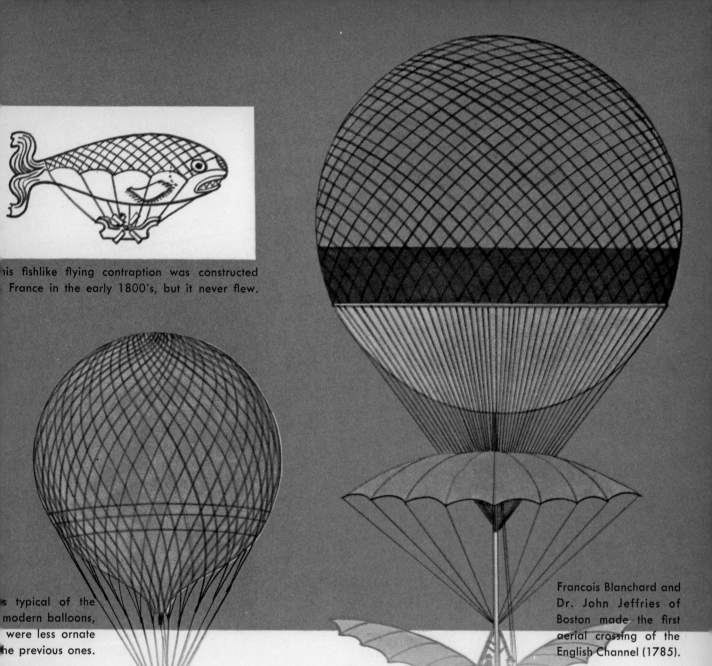

This fishlike flying contraption was constructed France in the early 1800's, but it never flew.

...s typical of the modern balloons, ...were less ornate ...the previous ones.

Francois Blanchard and Dr. John Jeffries of Boston made the first aerial crossing of the English Channel (1785).

Some sixteen years after Cavendish dis-covered his new gas, Joseph and Jacques Montgol-fier, French ornithoptists, were fasci-nated by watching smoke travel up from the fireplace through the chimney. They conceived the idea of making a smoke cloud which would fly in the air. They took a lightweight bag, filled it with smoke, and watched it float through the air.

How did the first balloonists fly?

After numerous experiments, they made a large linen bag, about 110 feet in circumference. At Annonay, in late 1783, they had the bag suspended over a fire of wool and straw in order to fill it with smoke. The smoke-filled bag rose almost 6,000 feet into the air and stayed afloat for 10 minutes. It fell to earth, as the heated gas inside the bag cooled, landing a couple of miles away. A man-made object had actually flown.

With the French Royal Academy of Sciences, the brothers built a larger bal-loon, 41 feet in diameter. It carried

9

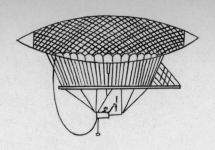

Henri Giffard built the first successful dirigible (top left) in 1852. It was powered by a propeller driven by a steam engine. The first controllable dirigible (above) was built by Alberto Santos-Dumont. Barrage balloons (left) were used in World Wars I and II to prevent low-level flying attacks by enemy planes.

some 400 to 500 pounds into the air, thus proving that it was possible to lift a man. On September 19, 1783, the new balloon carried its first passengers — a duck, a rooster and a sheep, and returned them safely to earth. Less than one month later, the first human ascent was made. Jean Francois Pilâtre de Rozier stayed aloft for over 4 minutes and reached a height of almost 85 feet.

Shortly after Pilâtre de Rozier took the first balloon flight, J. A. C. Charles, a French physicist, filled a rubber-coated silk balloon with hydrogen, which Cavendish had discovered. This balloon rose more rapidly than the earlier ones, remained in flight for almost 45 minutes, and landed over 16 miles away. Professor Charles raced after the balloon, but when he arrived he found the peasants using pitchforks to kill the unknown "monster."

Why did the hydrogen balloon fly?

The *Charlière,* as hydrogen balloons were called for many years, rose rapidly

because hydrogen is considerably lighter than smoke or air. The weight of the air in a balloon that is about 3½ feet in diameter is 8 pounds. The weight of hydrogen in a similar balloon is only ½ pound.

The greatest of the early balloonists was

Who were other famous early balloonists?

Francois Blanchard, who demonstrated balloon flying all over Europe and made the first American balloon flight on January 9, 1793. His most famous flight was across the English Channel in 1785, when he established the first international air mail on record.

Another famous early balloonist was Captain Coutelle of the French Revolutionary Army, who manned the first

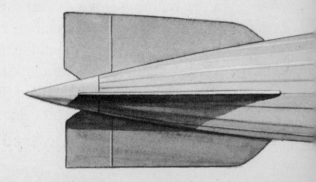

The zeppelin had a metal frame in which "bags" of hydrogen were used to make the craft "float."

balloon used in warfare. In 1794, at the battle of Fleurus, the captain signaled information to General Jourdan, who was able to take advantage of the shifting battle situation and emerged victorious.

The early balloons consisted of an inflated bag to which an open basket, or *gondola* (GON-do-la), was attached by ropes. To make the balloon go higher into the air, the "pilot" lightened its weight by dropping bags of sand, which were secured to the sides of the gondola. To make the balloon descend, he opened a valve and let some of the gas escape. The balloon rose into the air, but there was no way to control its flight. Once aloft, the balloon — and the men with it — were at the mercy of the winds.

How does a dirigible differ from a balloon?

The *dirigible* (DIR-i-gi-ble), or airship as it is sometimes called, can be steered. It consists of an elongated, gas-filled bag with cars, or gondolas, below for passengers and power. The dirigible takes advantage of the wind, but also uses motor-driven propellers. The early dirigibles used a sliding weight to make them go up or down. Pushing the weight toward the front pointed the nose of the airship down; conversely, with the weight toward the back, the nose pointed upward. Later dirigibles used horizontal tail fins to direct their upward and downward movement. Vertical tail fins were used to steer them right and left.

When did the first dirigible fly?

In 1852, almost seventy years after the first Montgolfier balloon rose over Annonay, a French engineer, Henri Giffard, built the first successful dirigible. Shaped like a cigar, it was 143 feet long and was powered by a 3-horsepower steam engine with a propeller attached to the gondola. Because of its low speed, under 5 miles per hour, this airship was pushed backward in a strong wind.

The first dirigible which could be accurately controlled and guided was *Airship Number One,* built by Alberto Santos-Dumont, a Brazilian millionaire living in France. In 1901, he flew his airship around the Eiffel Tower in Paris.

What is a zeppelin?

The early dirigibles were nonrigid; that is, they were long gas-filled bags. A gondola and powered propeller were attached. When longitudinal framing, running the length of the bag, was used as reinforcement, the semi-rigid dirigible was created.

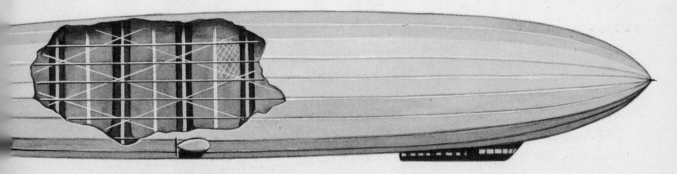

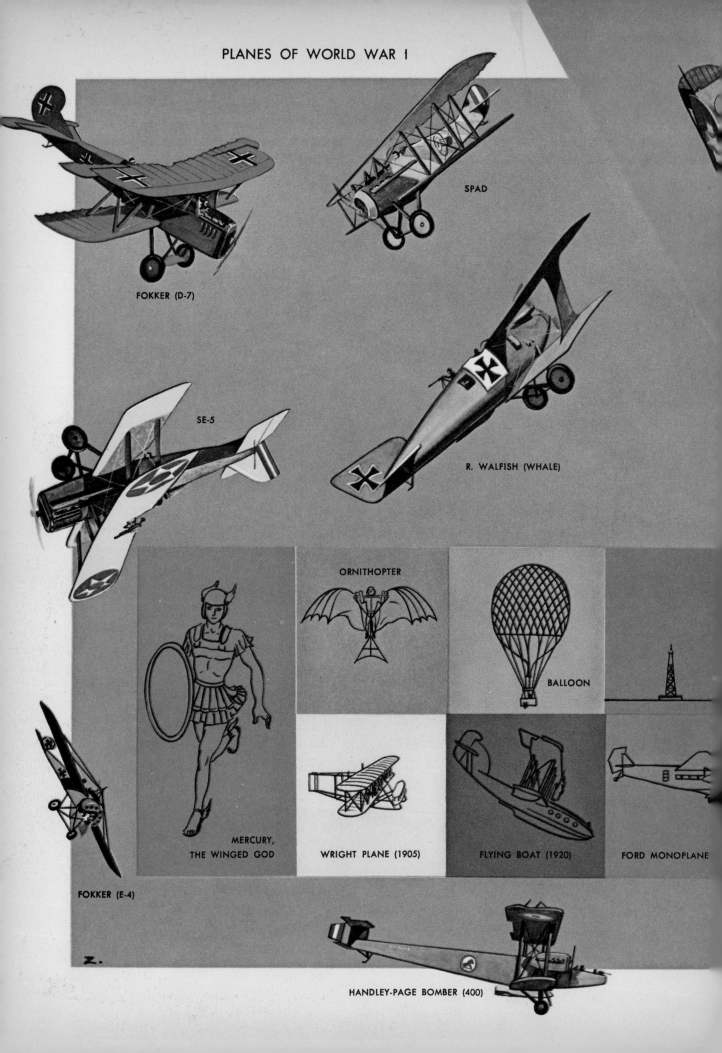

PLANES OF WORLD WAR I

FOKKER (D-7)

SPAD

SE-5

R. WALFISH (WHALE)

ORNITHOPTER

BALLOON

MERCURY,
THE WINGED GOD

WRIGHT PLANE (1905)

FLYING BOAT (1920)

FORD MONOPLANE

FOKKER (E-4)

Z.

HANDLEY-PAGE BOMBER (400)

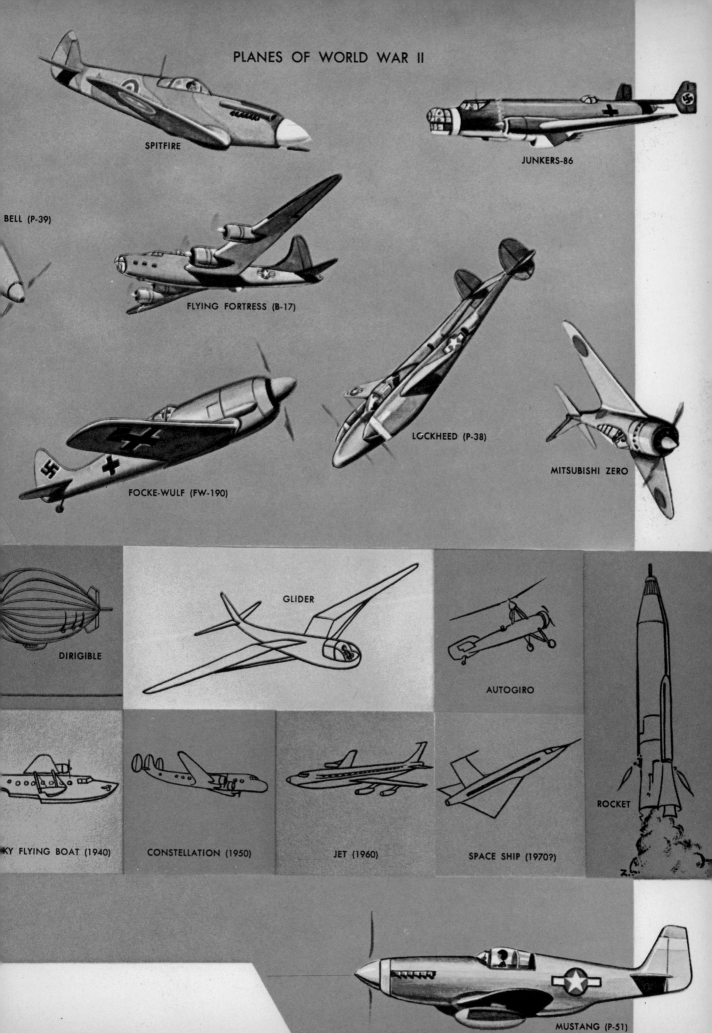

PLANES OF WORLD WAR II

SPITFIRE

JUNKERS-86

BELL (P-39)

FLYING FORTRESS (B-17)

LOCKHEED (P-38)

MITSUBISHI ZERO

FOCKE-WULF (FW-190)

DIRIGIBLE

GLIDER

AUTOGIRO

ROCKET

KY FLYING BOAT (1940)

CONSTELLATION (1950)

JET (1960)

SPACE SHIP (1970?)

MUSTANG (P-51)

The rigid dirigible, or *zeppelin* (ZEP-pe-lin), was first built by Count Ferdinand von Zeppelin of Germany in 1899. This type, as contrasted with the non-rigid and semi-rigid, had a complete rigid framework covered with fabric. Inside the frame were several gas-filled balloons, and below the frame was a cabin for the crew. It was 155 feet long and 40 feet in diameter.

During World War I, the Germans used zeppelins to drop bombs from the sky. After the war, other countries, including the United States, began to build zeppelin-type airships. In 1919, the British R-34 made the first trans-atlantic airship flight between England and the United States.

In 1929, the Graf Zeppelin took about ten days (flying time), traveling almost 22,000 miles, to go completely around the earth. Bigger and faster zeppelins were built, and they carried passengers, freight and mail to many sections of the world. The largest of these was the *Hindenburg* which was 830 feet long and 135 feet in diameter.

Two factors contributed to the decline of the zeppelins. First, those filled with hydrogen were very dangerous, since hydrogen explodes and burns. The last hydrogen-filled zeppelin seen outside of Germany was the *Hindenburg*, which exploded and burned in May, 1937, while landing at Lakehurst, New Jersey.

Why did the zeppelin disappear?

Although the United States used *helium* (HE-li-um), a natural gas which does not burn, its airships, the *Akron* and *Macon*, were both lost. They were destroyed by bad weather, the second factor which caused the decline of zeppelin-type airships.

Small, nonrigid airships, or blimps, are still used for offshore anti-submarine patrol duty and to explore the edges of space, but large, rigid airships are part of history.

The Air Pioneers

Sir George Cayley has been called the father of *aeronautics* (aer-o-NAU-tics). This is the science of flight, including the principles and techniques of building and flying balloons, airships and airplanes, as well as *aerodynamics* (aer-o-dy-NAM-ics), the science of air in motion and the movement of bodies through the air.

Who is the father of aeronautics?

This early nineteenth century Englishman denounced ornithopters as impractical. Drawing upon an earlier discovery, Cayley decided that it would be possible to make a plane fly through the air if the plane were light enough, and if air could be forced against its wings by moving the plane through the air.

He solved the problem of making the

plane light by using diagonal bracing to reinforce the wings and body instead of using solid pieces of wood. The second problem, moving the ship through the air, was to be solved by a propeller-driven engine. Since there was no engine light enough or powerful enough, Cayley designed his own. It was an internal combustion engine which would use "oil of tar," or gasoline, as we now call it. But the fuel was too costly and Cayley was forced to abandon his engine. It was not until almost a hundred years later that such an engine was successfully built.

Sir George Cayley, father of aeronautics, built a successful glider in 1804, but he was unable to build a powered aircraft. His designs, however, were good.

Powered flight really started with William Henson and John Stringfellow.

When did the first powered airplane fly?

Using Cayley's principles, these two Englishmen designed an *aerial steam carriage* in 1842. Many of their ideas were practical, but they, too, were ahead of their time — there was no adequate engine.

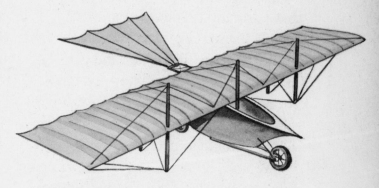

In 1848, Stringfellow, working alone, built a model 10 feet long with a batlike wing. It had an engine which weighed less than 9 pounds and powered two propellers. It made short, sustained flights, flying as much as 40 yards. It was only a model, but it was real, powered flight.

The immediate ancestor of the successful powered airplane was the glider. It is a heavier-than-air machine *without* an engine. The glider uses air currents to sustain its flight. In calm weather, it can be launched

How does a glider fly?

Powered flight came closer to reality with William Samuel Henson and John Stringfellow. They designed and flew the first powered models. But they were unable to build an engine to power a full-size plane.

from a high hilltop to obtain the needed forward thrust. The air rushing past its wings creates the necessary upward lift to counteract the gravitational force. The glider floats on the air and gradually descends to the ground.

In strong winds, the glider can be launched uphill so that it is picked up by the strong currents. It soars into the sky and continues to fly until the wind currents can no longer sustain it.

The greatest contribution in this field was made by Otto and Gustav Lilienthal. While still in high school in Germany, Otto built his first glider. It had wings that measured 6 by 3 feet each. In 1891, in Anklam, Germany, Otto made the first successful glider flight.

The brothers, noticing that birds took off *into* the wind, did the same with their gliders. They built many monoplane (single wing) and biplane (double wing) gliders and made over two thousand successful flights.

Perhaps Otto Lilienthal could have flown an airplane if a successful engine were available. In his attempt to develop such an engine, Otto lost his life. His experimental engine failed in flight and the airplane crashed.

Who made the first successful powered flight? Professor Langley, mathematician, physicist and Director of the Smithsonian Institution in Washington, D. C., was the last great air pioneer who failed to fly a plane. Using models, he supplied the answers to several problems which had to be solved before flying could be successful.

Early in the Spanish-American War, President McKinley asked Langley to develop a flying machine. Langley's assistant, Charles Manly, designed and built the first radial engine — the cylinders are built in a circle around the crankshaft. The engine used gasoline as fuel — it was Cayley's dream come true, almost a hundred years later.

Langley's *aerodrome* (AER-o-drome), as he called his plane, failed to fly on its second test on October 7, 1903. But some two months later, on December 17, 1903, at Kitty Hawk, North Carolina, the Wright brothers made the first successful flight.

Wilbur and Orville Wright were bicycle manufacturers from Dayton, Ohio, who built and flew gliders as early as 1900. After extensive work

The brothers Otto and Gustav Lilienthal paved the way for modern aviation. They built many gliders which flew successfully, and attempted powered flight. Otto was killed while testing a glider to which was attached a motor run by carbon dioxide.

on models, tested in wind tunnels, the Wright brothers designed and built their engine — a 4-cylinder model, weighing about 200 pounds, which developed 16 horsepower. They mounted this engine in a reinforced glider, and at Kitty Hawk, Orville Wright made four successful flights in one day. The first lasted only 12 seconds during which time the plane flew 120 feet. On the fourth flight the plane covered 852 feet and remained in the air for 59 seconds.

Despite its advanced engine, Samuel Langley's plane failed to fly. The gasoline engine, weighing less than three pounds per horsepower, was unequaled for twenty years.

The Wright brothers worked in Dayton for five years after their success at Kitty Hawk. In 1908, they developed a military airplane for the U. S. Army and in 1909, they demonstrated that a plane was capable of carrying a passenger. It flew at 40 miles per hour, carrying enough gasoline for a flight of 125 miles.

How did early aviation progress?

All over Europe and America, successful airplanes were demonstrated. In 1909, Louis Blériot flew across the English Channel. In that same year, the first international air meet was held at Rheims, France with thirty-eight airplanes participating. At that meet, Glenn H. Curtis, an American airplane designer and builder, established the speed record of 47.8 miles per hour. Hubert Latham, an Englishman, set the altitude record of 508 feet, while Henri Farman, a Frenchman, established the endurance record of 3 hours and 5 min-

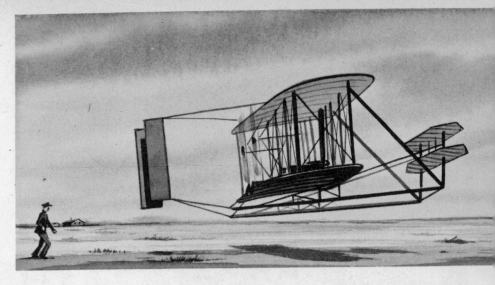

On December 17, 1903, at Kitty Hawk, North Carolina, the first heavier-than-air plane was flown by the Wrights.

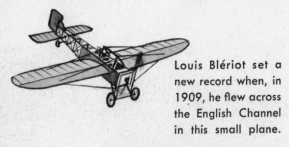

Louis Blériot set a new record when, in 1909, he flew across the English Channel in this small plane.

The first plane to take off and land on a ship at sea was flown by Eugene Ely, an American (1910).

utes. The longest flight at the meet was 118 miles.

One year later, in 1910, Eugene Ely, an American pilot, demonstrated a flight which eventually led to aircraft carriers. His plane took off from the cruiser *U.S.S. Birmingham* and landed on the battleship *U.S.S. Pennsylvania*.

The outbreak of World War I spurred the development of the airplane. Although attention was concentrated on the plane as a military weapon, it helped to establish aviation, train pilots, foster aircraft manufacturing and increase the public's awareness of aviation's possibilities.

Many men took to flying. They bought surplus Government airplanes, and earned their living doing stunt flying and taking people up for short flights around airports. These men were the so-called "gypsies" and "barnstormers" who helped aviation to grow.

Glenn Curtis was not only a plane designer and pilot, but also a manufacturer. All his planes were named after birds—*Hawk, Eagle, Condor, Falcon* and *Robin*.

The NC-4 prov 1919, that a ocean expanse not limit travel b

In May 1919, the NC-4 made aviation

How did airplanes "shrink" the world? history by crossing the Atlantic. The Navy had three patrol bombers, flying boats which could take off and land only in water. Each plane carried a crew of five: two pilots, a radio operator, an engineer and a reserve engineer-pilot. Only the NC-4 completed the journey from Rockaway, Long Island to Plymouth, England, a distance of 3,936 miles. Some fifty destroyers lined the Atlantic to act as guides for the planes and to be ready to help any that were in distress. The total flying time was 52½ hours, not including the time necessary at the seven stops for refueling and repairs.

In 1924, the Army sent its Douglas biplane bombers on a flight around the world. Four planes left Seattle, Washington on April 6. On September 28, only two — the *Chicago* and the *New Orleans* — returned. They had crossed twenty-eight countries, covered 26,345

Some 33 hours and 30 minutes after he took off from Roosevelt Field in Long Island, Lindbergh landed his *Spirit of St. Louis* at Le Bourget, an airfield outside of Paris.

Two Douglas World Cruisers carried their Army flight crews in the first round-the-world flight in 1924.

During parts of their trip, the landing wheels were replaced by pontoons.

miles, and crossed the Pacific for the first time. The actual flying time was about 15½ days.

The race from New York to Paris was

Who made the first nonstop solo flight across the Atlantic? spurred by a $25,000 prize which Raymond Orteig, French-born owner of a New York hotel, offered to the first one to make the flight nonstop. Although Orteig offered this money in 1919, it was not until 1926 that Rene Founck, a famous French aviator of World War I, made the first try. His plane crashed at take-off.

Many others tried and failed. It was Captain Charles A. Lindbergh, a former mail pilot, Army officer and barnstormer, who finally claimed the prize. Financed by a group of St. Louis businessmen, Lindbergh had Ryan Aircraft of San Diego build a special monoplane with a Wright J-5 Whirlwind engine at a cost of $10,580. The builders at Ryan worked as many as eighteen hours a day to complete the plane in sixty days.

Lindbergh brought his plane, *The Spirit of St. Louis,* to Roosevelt Field, Long Island where, despite the fog and drizzle, he took off at 7:52 A.M. on May 20, 1927. To make room for extra gasoline, Lindbergh flew alone. To make the plane lighter, he carried no parachute and removed the radio and all other "surplus" equipment and charts.

Alone, with no radio, Lindbergh plowed through rain, sleet, fog and high winds across the Atlantic, flew over Ireland and England and on over France. He circled the Eiffel Tower and landed nearby at the airport of Le Bourget, on May 21 at 10:22 P.M., Paris time. He had flown over 3,600 miles in 33 hours and 30 minutes.

The "Lone Eagle," as Lindbergh was called, was greeted by large, enthusiastic crowds. He received wild welcomes everywhere he went. The world was talking about "Lucky Lindy" — and aviation.

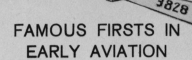

FAMOUS FIRSTS IN EARLY AVIATION

The first air-mail service was established by the U. S. Post Office between New York and Washington, D. C. on May 15, 1918. Major Reuben Fleet piloted the first flight and Lieutenant George Boyle made the return flight.

* * *

The first nonstop transatlantic flight was made by Captain John Alcock and Lieutenant Arthur Brown of England in a Vickers-Vimy biplane on June 14, 1919. They flew from Newfoundland to Clifdon, Ireland in 16 hours and 12 minutes.

* * *

The first nonstop transcontinental flight from New York to San Diego was made by Lieutenants Oakley Kelly and John Macready in May, 1923. Their trip in a Fokker T-2 took 26 hours and 50 minutes.

* * *

The first airplane flight over the North Pole was made on May 9, 1926. Lieutenant Floyd Bennett piloted a trimotor Fokker, commanded by Commander Richard E. Byrd, from Spitzbergen, Norway. During the 15 hours, before the plane returned to its base, it flew over the Pole.

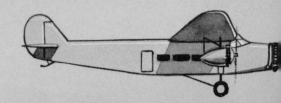

Da Vinci designed a helixpteron, the first helicopter.

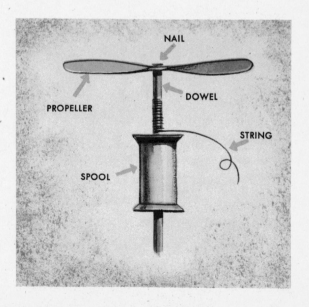

The Launoy, or Chinese flying top, was the first successful model of a heavier-than-air machine that man built. It was the basis for the development of copters.

Flying in Any Direction

A helicopter can fly in any direction — straight up, straight down, forward, backward, sideways — and it can even stand still in mid-air. Furthermore, the helicopter can creep along a few inches above the ground or water, or it can climb thousands of feet into the sky and travel at over 100 miles per hour.

How did the helicopter originate? The fifteenth century genius, Leonardo da Vinci, not only designed a workable parachute and the ornithopter, but he also designed a very special flying machine. Overhead, it had a large screw-shaped propeller, which da Vinci hoped would screw into the air and lift the machine. He called this flying machine the *helixpteron* (hel-i-TER-on), which comes from the Greek *helix* (meaning "spiral") and *pteron* (meaning "wing").

For more than two hundred fifty years no one paid attention to this idea. But in 1783, the French naturalist Launoy "discovered" a Chinese flying top, a toy probably brought back from the Orient. The top was made of feathers, wood and string and it could fly straight up. It was the first man-made heavier-than-air object that could leave the ground on its own power.

This top inspired George Cayley and he built a similar one, but used tin for the blades instead of feathers. The Cayley top rose 90 feet into the air.

How can you make a Cayley top? All you need in order to make a Cayley top is a 6-inch model airplane propeller, an empty spool, a dowel that just about slides through the hole in the spool and a piece of string about 2 feet long.

Nail the propeller to one end of the dowel. Wind the string around the

SPOOL · PROPELLER · NAIL · DOWEL · STRING

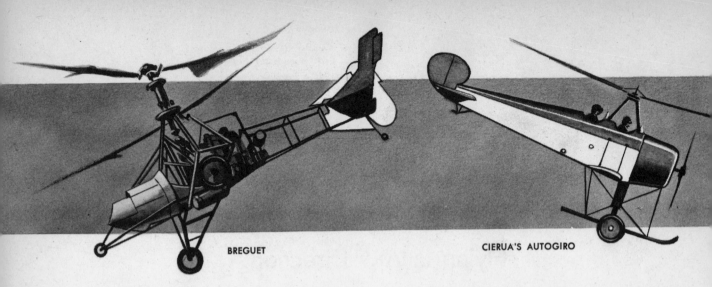

BREGUET

CIERUA'S AUTOGIRO

dowel, about an inch below the propeller. Then, slide the dowel into the spool. Hold the spool in one hand with the propeller pointing straight up. Pull the string hard and quickly with the other hand. The propeller spins and lifts the dowel straight into the air.

In 1878, Enrico Forlanini, using a pow-

Who were the early helicopter builders?

erful, tiny steam engine he designed and built, made a model helicopter. This steam-driven model hovered in the air at about 40 feet for 20 seconds. It provided positive proof that such a flying machine was possible.

The first full-sized helicopter to fly was built by Louis Breguet in 1907. This plane rose some 5 feet off the ground, but it could not be controlled and was unstable. It was not until 1922 that Russian-born George de Bothezat built and flew a helicopter that was stable and controllable. His *Flying Octopus,* built as a military helicopter, was an enormous ship with four rotors or horizontal blades. Although it made over one hundred successful flights from McCook Field in the United States, it was abandoned because it was too clumsy and complicated.

The *autogyro* (auto-GY-ro) is a hybrid,

How does an autogyro fly?

a combination of an airplane and helicopter. Its Spanish inventor, Juan de la Cierva, used a small biplane and attached a set of whirling blades on top of the plane. There was no engine to work the top blades. They turned as the air from the propeller rushed passed them.

The turning of the rotary blades gave the plane extra lift or upward pull. For this reason, it was possible for the plane to take off at a slower engine speed and get into the air in less time. It appeared to jump into the air at take-off.

The autogyro's whirling blades turned only when the plane's propeller was spinning and, therefore, it hovered in the air. The only advantage of the autogyro was its ability to get into the air quickly at a lower engine speed. Although the autogyro has disappeared from the sky, the development of flexible rotary blades by Juan de la Cierva helped make it possible to build truly successful helicopters.

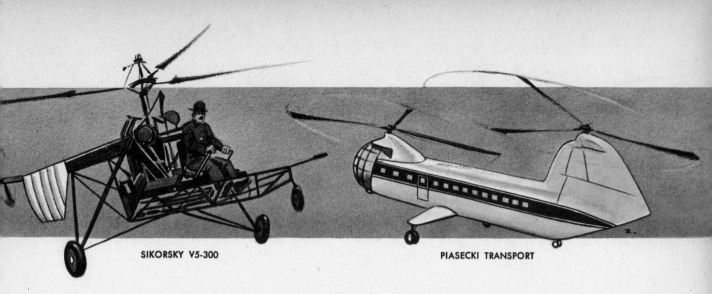

SIKORSKY V5-300

PIASECKI TRANSPORT

One man stands out in the history of helicopters — Igor Sikorsky. As a young man in Kiev, Russia, he built a model helicopter in 1910. He continued to study the experiments of others and in 1939, working in the United States, he decided to try again.

Who perfected the helicopter?

For months, he worked on "Igor's Nightmare," as many people called his helicopter. He conducted many experiments and in May, 1940, he tried his first free flight. It was an overwhelming success compared with anything that preceded it. His ship could fly up, down, backward, sideways, and could hover in the air. But his ship had difficulty in flying forward. Additional work solved this problem and he started to produce workable helicopters.

World War II spurred the development of helicopters and in 1943, eighteen-year-old Stanley Hiller, Jr. designed and built the first coaxial helicopter. He used one engine to turn both rotors.

The helicopter now has many uses. It is used to spray chemicals over crops to protect them from insects, to fight forest fires, to carry mail, to inspect power lines and pipe lines in rugged mountain country. It is also used in land- and sea-rescue work, by cowboys on very large ranches, and even acts as a "bus" between airports.

The rotor blades over the helicopter lift the ship and make it fly. The blades act somewhat like the wings of an airplane. The pilot of a helicopter can tilt these blades — this tilt is called *pitch*. Tilting the moving blades creates lift. If you have ever flown a kite, you know how this works. The kite is tilted in the air, held in that position by the string you hold in your hand. The moving air passes the tilted kite, lifts it and keeps it flying. But if you let go of the string, the kite is no longer tilted, and it will glide down to the ground.

How does the helicopter fly?

To climb into the air, the pilot tilts the moving blades and the helicopter goes straight up. When he wants to come down, he decreases the tilt, or pitch, of the blades. This decreases the lift, and gravity brings the ship down. If he wants to hover or stand still in the air, he sets the pitch of the blades so that the upward lift equals the pull toward the ground. Now, picture these moving blades as a saucer. You can tilt the entire saucer in any direction. It is through this tilting that the pilot can make the plane go forward, backward or sideways.

There is a smaller set of blades near the tail of the helicopter, nicknamed a "pinwheel." These blades also revolve and their pitch can be changed as well. By controlling their pitch, the pilot can keep the ship straight or make right and left turns.

Modern aviation has made it possible for man to fly like a bird. A miniature heli-copter is capable of carrying one man. He can fly straight up, sideways, forward, backward, downward or hover in the air. The personal *whirlywings* have been used experimentally by the U. S. Army for its scouts.

How do the modern ornithopters fly?

This is a U. S. Army craft — a whirlywing.

The *aerocycle* is another version of a one-man helicopter. This experimental model, also used by the Army, is somewhat larger than a *whirlywing* and the man stands on top of the cycle to fly it through the air.

Another small, one-man flying machine is the *flying platform*. It is shaped like a large doughnut and has a fan in

FLYING PLATFORM

the center. This fan lifts and propels the platform on which the man stands. The pilot's "leaning" controls the horizontal flight of this craft.

Picture an airplane, higher than a three-story building, standing on its tail. The propeller starts turning and soon the plane goes straight up into the air. Once the

What is VTOL?

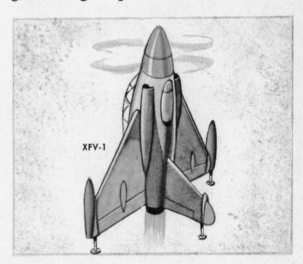

XFV-1

pilot gets up as high as he wants to go, he straightens out the plane and it flies like any ordinary airplane. Such planes as the Lockheed XFV-1 and the Con-vair XFY-1, often called "flying pogo sticks," are VTOL aircraft. VTOL means "vertical take-off and landing."

Although these planes are like conventional, horizontal flying craft, they act like helicopters in some ways. Not only can they take off and land vertically, but they can hover in the air as well. These experimental planes can take off and land from practically any place — the top of a building, the deck of a ship or in rugged mountain country studded with trees. Once aloft, they are high-speed aircraft and can exceed 500 miles per hour.

Theory and Facts of Flight

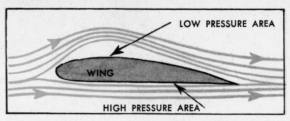

As the air rushes past the wing, or airfoil, it flows above and below the airfoil. The shape of the airfoil causes the air to travel a greater distance over the top of the foil. This results in a lowering of air pressure, which creates an upward lift on the airfoil.

Why does an airplane fly? About forty years before the American Revolution, a Swiss scientist, Daniel Bernoulli, discovered that in any moving fluid the pressure is lowest where the speed is greatest. The air about us acts like a fluid and if we can increase the speed of air over a surface, such as a wing, the pressure should decrease and the wing should rise.

In actual practice, the wing of an airplane is shaped somewhat like a bow — the upper surface is curved while the lower part is straight. Since the air has to travel a greater distance over the top part of the wing, it must travel at a faster speed. As a result, the pressure is lower above the wing than below it and the wing rises, or *lifts*, into the air.

When an airplane flies horizontally, its propeller must do two things. First, it must keep the plane from falling and, second, it must overcome the friction of the air in order to pull the plane forward. The turning propeller increases the speed of the air over the wings. According to the Bernoulli principle, this creates *lift* — the upward pressure on the wing. Lift overcomes *gravity* — the downward pressure created by the weight of the plane.

The propeller slices through the air in the same way that a screw cuts into wood, and pulls the plane forward. This forward motion of the propeller is called *thrust*. It counteracts the *drag* of the atmosphere, the force that resists forward motion.

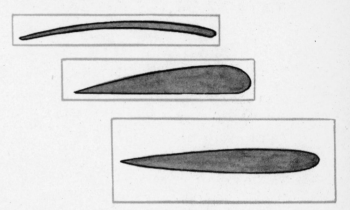

Airfoil cross sections, top to bottom: Design used by Wright brothers; "high-light" wing used on small planes; "high-speed" wing used by commercial liners.

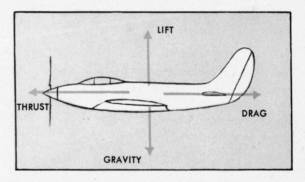

These four forces act upon a plane while in flight.

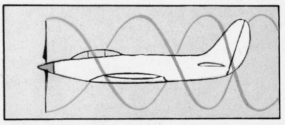

The propeller, called airscrews in England, provides the forward pulling or lifting power of an airplane.

An airplane, like any moving object following the basic laws of physics, tends to continue in a straight line unless some force is exerted to change its direction. The speed at which the engine turns the propeller is governed by the *throttle*. Opening the throttle increases the air speed and lifts the plane higher.

What makes an airplane go up and down?

Equally important is the *elevator* which controls the plane's upward and downward movement. It is a horizontal, hinged surface attached to the tail. When the pilot applies back pressure on the control stick, or column, the elevator is tilted upward. The air, striking the raised elevator, forces the tail down and the wing upward. The thrust of the propeller pulls the plane upward. Conversely, when the pilot pushes the control stick forward, the elevator is tilted downward. This forces the tail up and the wing down.

Two parts of an airplane control its turns to the right and left. The *rudder,* a vertical surface that is hinged to the tail, swings the tail to the right or left just in the same way as a section of the tail swings up or down. On the ground, it is used to make the plane turn just as a rudder of a boat does. In the air, however, the major purpose of the rudder is *not* to make the plane turn, but to assist the plane in entering and recovering from a turn.

How does an airplane turn?

The *ailerons,* small sections of the rear edge of the wing, near the tips, are hinged and are so connected that as one rises, the other lowers. This action tends to raise one wing and lower the other.

When the aileron on the right wing is lowered, the right wing rises and the plane will be tilted, or *banked,* to the left. The lifting force on the right wing is no longer completely upward — part of the force is pulling the plane to the left. This, in combination with the rudder, produces a left turn; that is, the plane is "lifted" around the turn.

The propeller provides the power for the forward thrust. The elevators enable the pilot to make the plane go up or down. The flaps aid in the ascent and help provide a smoother descent. The ailerons and rudder help the plane to turn left and right.

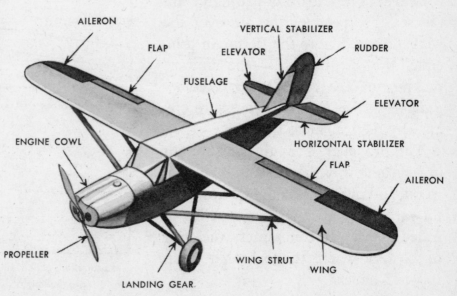

AILERON

FLAP

VERTICAL STABILIZER

ELEVATOR

RUDDER

FUSELAGE

ELEVATOR

ENGINE COWL

HORIZONTAL STABILIZER

FLAP

AILERON

PROPELLER

WING STRUT

WING

LANDING GEAR

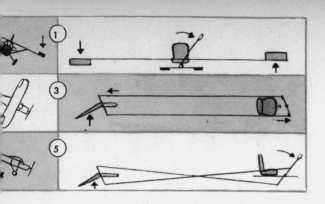
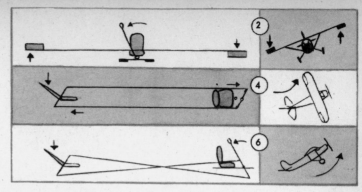

HOW TO FLY AN AIRPLANE

AILERONS (FRONT VIEW)	RUDDER (TOP VIEW)	ELEVATORS (SIDE VIEW)
1. LEFT STICK	3. RIGHT RUDDER	5. FORWARD STICK
2. RIGHT STICK	4. LEFT RUDDER	6. BACKWARD STICK

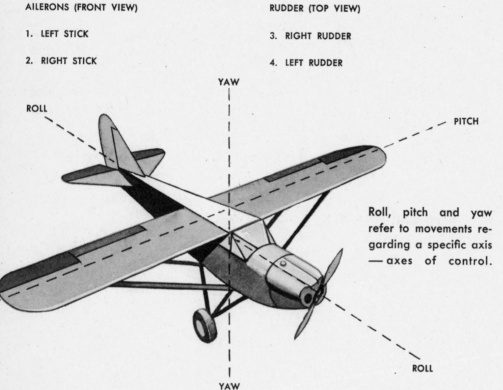

Roll, pitch and yaw refer to movements regarding a specific axis —axes of control.

How can you demonstrate *lift*? Take a piece of paper about 2 inches wide and about 5 inches long. Fold it an inch from the end. Hold the paper with your forefinger and thumb so that the fold is about an inch or two from your mouth. Blow with all your might over the top of the paper.

What happened? The paper moves up or *lifts*. By increasing the speed of the air over the top of the paper, you have reduced the pressure, causing the paper to rise.

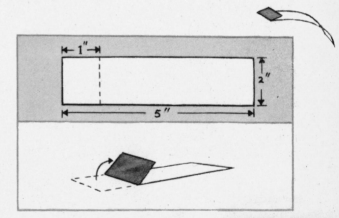

You can demonstrate lift, caused by the Bernoulli effect, on the upper surface of a piece of paper (right).

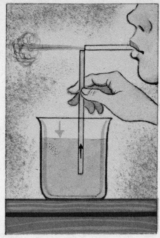

You can demonstrate this same principle with a simple atomizer. Blowing across the top of the tube — you can use a straw — reduces the pressure and causes the liquid to rise within the tube.

Take a 3 by 5 index card and fold a 1-inch section along the long edge upward at a 45-degree angle. Paste the card, along its short center line, to a piece of balsa wood

How can you demonstrate the working of an elevator?

about 10 inches long. Balance the wood with the attached card on a round pencil, like a seesaw. Mark this "balance" point and push a straight pin through the balsa so that it is parallel to the card.

Hold the pin lightly between the thumb and forefinger of both hands. Hold the balsa wood in front of your mouth with the card farthest away. Now when you blow with all your might, the raised portion of the index card acts like a plane's elevator. The front end of the balsa wood (nearest your mouth) will move upward, like the nose of a plane.

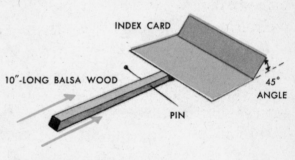

INDEX CARD

10"-LONG BALSA WOOD

PIN

45° ANGLE

DIRECTION FROM WHICH YOU BLOW

WHAT DO THE INSTRUMENTS TELL THE PILOT?

Here are only a few of the more important instruments which a pilot uses to guide his airplane:

Oil Pressure Gauge indicates the pressure of the oil in the engine. The dial is colored so that it is easier for the pilot to instantly spot any danger.

Oil Temperature Gauge tells the temperature of the oil in the engine.

Rate-of-Climb Indicator tells the pilot the speed at which his plane is climbing

or dropping. The indicator is at zero when the plane is flying level.

Air Speed Indicator notes how fast the plane is moving through the air. Four colors are used for greater safety. Red is used to show maximum speed at which the plane can fly. Yellow shows a caution range — speeds approaching maximum speed. Heavy blue is used for normal cruising speeds. Light blue is used to show landing speed.

Turn-and-Bank Indicator is actually two separate instruments. The curved glass tube with a metal ball in liquid, the bank indicator, located near the bottom of the instrument, shows whether the plane is tilted to the right or left. The turn indicator shows the direction in which the nose of the plane is headed — to the left, straight ahead or to the right.

Instrument Landing System Indicator helps the pilot land his plane when the airfield is covered by fog or very low clouds. When the two pointers line up with the white circles on the dial, the plane is directly on path approaching the runway for a perfect landing.

Fuel Gauge indicates how much gasoline the plane has in its tank.

Tachometer tells the pilot how his motor is doing. It indicates the number of revolutions of the engine or the speed at which the propellers are turning.

Altimeter shows the height of the plane above the ground. There are three pointers — the smallest shows height in tens of thousands of feet above the ground; the medium-sized pointer shows height in thousands of feet; and the longest pointer shows height in hundreds and parts of hundreds of feet. The altimeter pictured here shows an altitude, or height, of 14,750 feet.

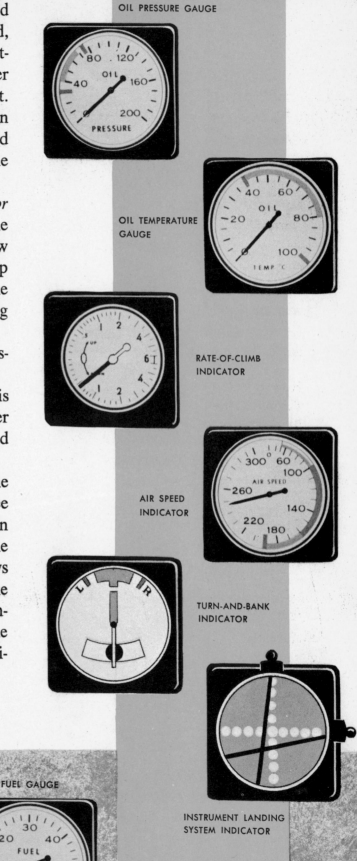

OIL PRESSURE GAUGE

OIL TEMPERATURE GAUGE

RATE-OF-CLIMB INDICATOR

AIR SPEED INDICATOR

TURN-AND-BANK INDICATOR

INSTRUMENT LANDING SYSTEM INDICATOR

ALTIMETER

TACHOMETER

FUEL GAUGE

Directional Gyro and Magnetic Compass are used to guide the plane. The magnetic compass acts like any regular compass you have seen — it points to the north. The directional gyro is used by the pilot to set his course. If the plane changes direction, the gyro shows this to the pilot.

Artificial Horizon helps a pilot when he is flying at night, in a cloud or in fog. During a clear day, a pilot keeps his plane straight and level by watching the horizon. At other times, he must use this instrument.

Drift Indicator is usually installed level with the floor. It shows the pilot how the wind might be blowing him off course.

In multi-engine, conventional aircraft, there is a separate oil pressure and oil temperature indicator and a tachometer for each engine. In addition, there is generally a separate fuel gauge for each tank in the plane. Thus, if you were to look at the panel of a large four-engine airliner which has six fuel

tanks, you would see seventeen more instruments than you see here. Furthermore, there is an identical set of dials for the co-pilot in addition to the pilot, and on some planes a third set of dials is used for the navigator-engineer.

Highways of the Air

There are thousands of airports of many different kinds throughout the world. In the United States, the Civil Aeronautics Administration (CAA) classifies the airports according to the length of their runways. An airport with a runway of 1,500 to 2,300 feet is classified as a personal airport and is used only by small, light, private planes.

DIRECTIONAL GYRO AND
MAGNETIC COMPASS

DRIFT INDICATOR

ARTIFICIAL HORIZON

Airports range from the small grass fields for two- and four-passenger planes to the very large fields with concrete runways that handle the large commercial jet airliners.

Airports where large domestic passenger airliners can land and take off must have runways of 6,000 to 7,000 feet. To meet the needs of today's large jetliners, some airports have runways of 10,000 feet or more, or about two miles.

In the air between the airports are

What are the airways? airways, or roads, through the sky along which the planes travel. Because of the many planes flying overhead, both during the day and night, it is necessary to set up rules for the road just as we have traffic rules for the cars on the streets.

Except when taking off or landing, airplanes must fly at least 500 feet above the ground. Over cities and other congested areas, the planes often have to fly 1,000 or even 2,000 feet above the ground.

The route a plane takes is determined by the CAA which controls all air traffic. At major airports, there are men sitting before air maps, radios and control boards, and they keep track of every plane as it plows through the skies.

Specific airways have been established to prevent planes from colliding in the air. All eastbound flights — planes flying from west to east — fly at *odd* thousand-foot levels, plus 500 feet, above sea level. Thus, a plane flying from Los Angeles to New York could fly at 15,500 feet. Westbound flights, on the other hand, fly at *even* thousand-foot levels, plus 500 feet, above sea level.

WHICH PLANE HAS THE RIGHT OF WAY?

Aircraft have rules that govern the right of way in the sky.

All flying craft have to give the right of way to a balloon.

Airplanes and airships have to give a glider the right of way.

An airplane must give an airship the right of way.

* * *

If two planes are flying so that their paths might cross, the plane to the right of the pilot has the right of way.

* * *

Should two planes be approaching head-on, both pilots must shift their planes to the right. As they pass, the planes must be at least 500 feet apart.

The same plane going from New York to Los Angeles could fly at 14,500 feet.

During a clear, sunny day — or Class C **How do air markers help pilots to fly?** weather according to the Air Weather Bureau — planes can fly by contact; that is, the pilot can see the ground and identify his route. There are various markers along the route on the ground. These markers also appear on special flight maps which the pilot carries with him just as we carry a road map in a car.

The air markers indicate location, have arrows pointing to the nearest air-

port and other identifying information. The markers are painted on highways, roofs of barns and factories, and the sides of high buildings such as grain elevators. They are also set in stone on mountains or in fields.

In addition to the visible markers, there is also radio contact. The CAA operates many radio stations throughout the country. By picking up different stations, the pilot can determine his exact position over the ground.

During the night, when it is clear, the pilot can spot visible ground markers, some of which are illuminated, special air beacons (similar to lights from a lighthouse) and airport lights and beacons.

Look into the cockpit of an airplane **How do pilots fly in all types of weather?** and you will see a maze of dials, knobs, switches and levers. These instruments and controls help the pilot at take-off, when he guides the plane safely through the airways and when he lands. Today's plane can land even when the pilot cannot see the airport.

The Instrument Landing System (ILS) is used when the airport's *ceiling* (the height from the ground to the clouds above) is too low for the pilot to land by sight. Through the use of electronic equipment, the pilot can "see" through the fog, rain, sleet and dark. A special instrument on his flight panel helps him align his airplane directly with the airport's runway. The instrument also shows him if he is too high or too low as he approaches.

Radar is also used to help pilots fly

through foul weather and to land safely. The major airports use Air Surveillance Radar (ASR) with which they can pinpoint the exact position in the sky of any plane within 60 miles of the airport. Some of the newer *blind landing* techniques (when the pilot cannot see the airport landing strip) involve automatic controls. The pilot sets the plane on special electronic instruments, and a ground controller, using radar, actually lands the plane.

Faster Than Sound

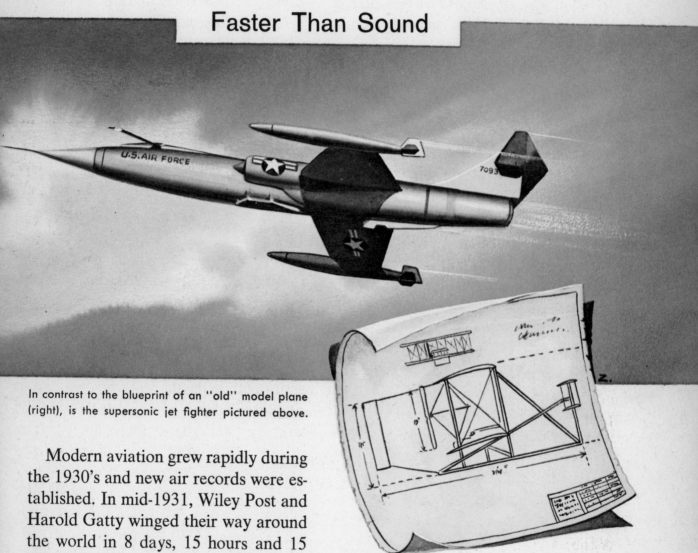

In contrast to the blueprint of an "old" model plane (right), is the supersonic jet fighter pictured above.

Modern aviation grew rapidly during the 1930's and new air records were established. In mid-1931, Wiley Post and Harold Gatty winged their way around the world in 8 days, 15 hours and 15 minutes. Two years later, Wiley Post set out by himself in his plane, the *Winnie Mae,* and made the same earth-circling trip in 7 days, 8 hours and 49 minutes. During this flight, he used two new aviation instruments — the radio compass and a robot or automatic pilot.

It has been said that the world was put on wings when the Douglas DC-3 was introduced in 1936. Until that time, the airlines used small planes, such as the Fokker trimotor and Ford trimotor. Each carried only eight people and reached top speeds of about 100 miles an hour. The DC-3 carried twenty-one passengers in addition to a crew of three, and it could fly at 180 miles per hour. This "workhorse of the airlines" helped to build air passenger travel in the United States.

The outbreak of World War II in September, 1939 signaled a new era in aviation history. Emphasis was placed on faster fighter planes, on larger bombers that could fly higher, and on troop transports that could carry more men and fly farther. World War II saw the first jet planes in real action.

The idea of jet power, or propulsion, goes back to early **When were jets first used?** history. The Greek mathematician, Hero, who lived in Alexandria about 130 B.C., is credited with being the first to build a jet engine. He converted steam pressure into jet action with an "engine" of his own design. It consisted

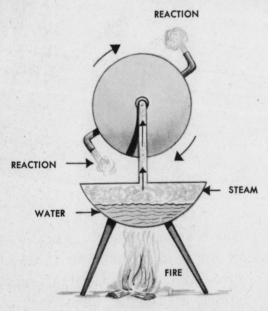

The "aeoliphile" was built by Hero of Alexandria.

of a hollow metal sphere which was mounted so that it could spin freely. The steam inside the sphere escaped through small nozzles, causing the sphere to spin. This engine was a scientific toy and was never put to use.

The jet principle was put to work during the Middle Ages in Europe. The *smoke-jack,* which some claim da Vinci invented, was used to turn a roasting spit in a fireplace. The turning action of the spit was produced by a fan in the chimney. The hot air passing up the chimney turned the fan.

In 1629, Giovanni Branca perfected a steam turbine using the jet principle to operate a milling machine. He used steam, which passed through a pipe, to turn a paddle-wheel similar to our modern turbines. The paddle-wheel operated the milling machine, crushing grain into flour.

Many other men worked on jet-powered machines over the years, and in 1926 an English scientist, Dr. Griffiths, proposed the use of jet-powered gas turbines to power an airplane. The first successful jet-plane flight was made in Germany when a Heinkel He-178 took to the air on August 27, 1939.

Have you ever pressed a spring together **How does a jet fly?** and let it go? What happens? It springs back to its original size. The air around us behaves in the same way. When you compress air, it tries to escape and expand to its original volume. When you heat air, it expands, and also tries to escape. Compressing and heating air give the jet engine its power.

If you take an inflated balloon and let it go, the air inside the balloon will escape. As it rushes out, the balloon "flies" through the air. This illustrates the principle which makes the jet fly. It is an example of Newton's third law of motion: "For every action, there is an equal and opposite reaction." As the air rushes out the back, the balloon goes forward.

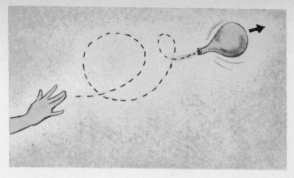

The balloon's activity is a form of jet propulsion.

There are several types of jet engines and all work on the same principle. A jet plane needs no propeller since it uses air to give it forward motion or thrust. The most common type of jet engine is the turbojet.

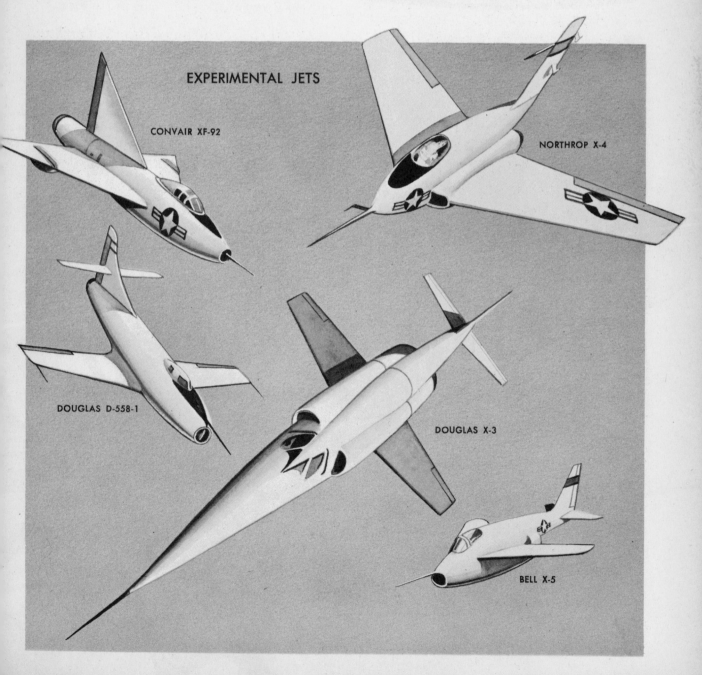

EXPERIMENTAL JETS

CONVAIR XF-92

NORTHROP X-4

DOUGLAS D-558-1

DOUGLAS X-3

BELL X-5

RAMJET AND PULSEJET

The *ramjet* is the simplest of all jet engines. It has no moving parts. The air is compressed by the forward motion of the plane. The plane has to be in motion *before* the ramjet works. Therefore, a plane with a ramjet engine has to be launched in the air by a "mother ship."

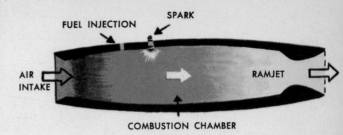

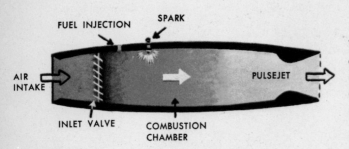

The *pulsejet* is also a simple jet engine. It has only one moving part, an inlet valve which controls the amount of air entering the engine. It was first used during World War II to power the V-1 flying bombs which the Germans rocketed into London, England.

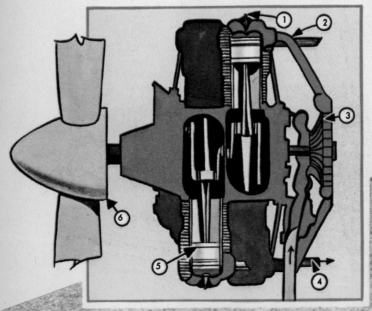

A reciprocating engine: (1) spark plug; (2) cylinder inlet; (3) shaft-driven supercharger; (4) cylinder exhaust; (5) piston; and (6) propeller.

Super aircraft require special aircraft facilities. One modern structure (below) is already built and in operation at Idlewild in N. Y.

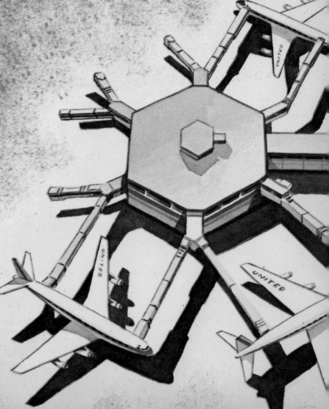

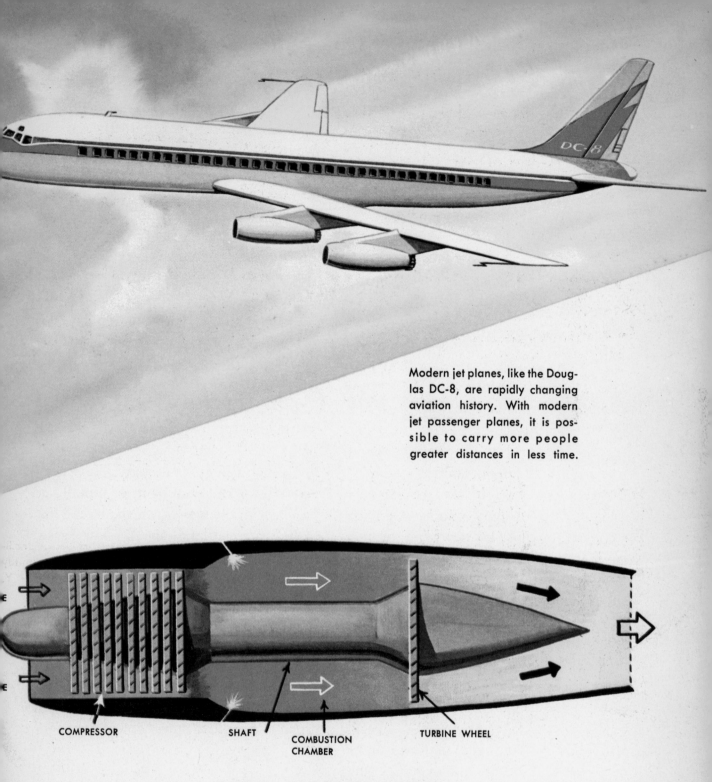

Modern jet planes, like the Douglas DC-8, are rapidly changing aviation history. With modern jet passenger planes, it is possible to carry more people greater distances in less time.

COMPRESSOR   SHAFT   COMBUSTION CHAMBER   TURBINE WHEEL

HOW A TURBOJET WORKS

1. Air is sucked into the engine through the front intake. The compressor, acting like a large fan, compresses the air and forces it through ducts, or tubes, to the combustion chamber.

2. In the combustion chamber, fuel is sprayed into the compressed air and ignited. The resulting hot gases expand rapidly and, with terrific force, blast their way out of the rear of the engine. This jet blast gives the engine and plane its forward thrust.

3. As the hot gases rush out of the engine, they pass through a set of blades, the turbine wheel. These blades react like a windmill and turn the main engine shaft, which operates the front compressor.

4. Some engines, designed to give extra pushing power, have an afterburner attached to the engine. This is a long tail cone in which more fuel is sprayed and burned, just before the gases pass through the rear exhaust.

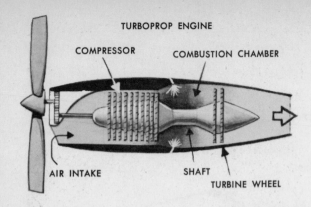

TURBOPROP ENGINE

COMPRESSOR   COMBUSTION CHAMBER

AIR INTAKE   SHAFT   TURBINE WHEEL

A *turboprop* is a jet engine connected to

Why do they use turboprops?

a conventional propeller. It combines the advantages of a gas turbine jet with those of a propeller. During take-off and low speeds, the propeller produces higher forward thrust. During landing, the propeller creates greater drag, enabling the plane to take off and land in shorter distances than a turbojet. However, the gas turbine jet is lightweight as compared with a conventional plane's piston motor and is without vibration in flight.

A turboprop, or *propjet* as it is also called, cannot fly as fast or as high as a turbojet. Turbojets are particularly suited for high-speed and high-altitude flights. On the other hand, propjets are more efficient at moderate altitudes than conventional piston-engine planes.

Have you ever noticed that during a

What is the sound barrier?

lightning storm you can see the flash of lightning before you hear the thunder? This is because light travels faster than sound. The speed of sound in freezing air (32°F.) is about 1,090 feet per second or 743 miles per hour. The speed of sound increases as the temperature rises, about a foot a second faster for each degree. At 68°F.,

the speed of sound in air is about 1,130 feet per second or 765 miles per hour.

Sound travels through the air in waves similar to those produced when you drop a stone into a pond. One of the people who studied sound and air waves was an Austrian professor of physics, Ernest Mach. About 1870, he photographed cannon shells flying through the air in order to discover what happens to an object as it speeds through the air. He found that the moving object produced *shock waves*. The object pushes against the molecules in the air. As one molecule is pushed, it in turn pushes the others near it. Imagine a long line of boys standing one behind the other. The last boy in the line gets pushed. As he moves forward, he pushes the boy in front of him. This happens all the way down the line. This is how sound and shock waves are produced.

As the speed of a plane approaches the speed of sound, it is pushing rapidly against the molecules in the air and creating shock waves. As the plane reaches the same speed as sound, these waves pile up and form an invisible barrier. When the plane exceeds the speed of sound, it must "crash" through

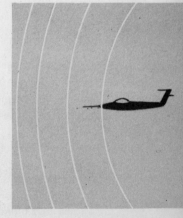

As the plane goes through the air, it creates sound waves. The plane itself displaces air about it as it speeds forward.

this barrier. As it does, it creates a thunderlike sound. You will see the plane before you hear its motor, just as you see lightning before you hear the thunder.

How did the sound barrier change the shape of planes? Slow-flying planes were never affected by air waves. As planes began to fly higher and faster, some pilots found that they encountered difficulties — the planes vibrated fiercely and the pilots couldn't operate the controls. What these pilots encountered was *wave drag;* that is, the piling-up of air in front of the plane — the sound barrier. Scientists and airmen studied this effect on planes and soon recognized what was happening.

To honor the man who first explored this subject scientifically, we measure the speed of a plane or rocket in *Mach numbers.* Aeronautical engineers use Mach 1 as equal to 680 miles per hour, the speed of sound at about 35,000 feet and higher, where the temperature is 50° or lower. Mach 2 equals twice the speed of sound or 1,360 miles per hour.

They found that the shock waves which caused wave drag were shaped like a cone. If the plane has long wings, it tends to spin more easily. As a result, jet planes, designed to fly faster than sound, have shorter wings set farther back along the sides of the body.

Scientists have studied sound waves and plane speeds in special wind tunnels using model planes, and thus, have helped engineers to develop better planes.

Why do planes fly in the jet stream? As planes climbed higher into the air, meteorologists (weather men) and pilots discovered fast-moving "rivers of air" between 35,000 and 55,000 feet above the earth. These rivers generally flow in an east-west direction and reach speeds as high as 450 miles per hour. Since the jet planes were the first to

As the plane's speed is increased, approaching at the speed of sound, it is increasing the compression of the sound waves.

As the speed of the plane exceeds that of the waves it created, it then plunges headlong through the sound barrier.

reach such high altitudes, these "rivers" became known as the *jet stream*.

A plane flying in the same direction as the jet stream is carried along in much the same way as you are carried by a strong wind when you are walking with it on a very windy day. A plane flying 600 miles per hour with the jet stream traveling 300 miles per hour, is actually traveling 900 miles an hour over the earth. The jet stream helps conserve fuel and shorten flying time.

What will future jet planes be like?

Revolutions in jet plane design are already taking place. One of the ships that North American Aviation is building is the B-70, half plane and half spaceship. This versatile craft, with a 156-foot pencil-thin body, is planned as a nuclear bomber with a range of 7,000 miles. As a passenger ship, it could carry 150 people at over 2,000 miles per hour, and fly nonstop from San Francisco to London.

Another remarkable change is the development of an airbreathing aircraft wing by Dr. Werner Pfenninger. As the conventional aircraft wing slices through the air at supersonic speeds, the air around the wing becomes choppy or turbulent. This turbulence creates a drag on the wing, causing the plane to slow up. With the new wing design, there will be a smooth flow of air over and under the wing. This smoother flight will require less fuel so that planes will be able to fly about fifty per cent farther without refueling. Two pilot models of this type of aircraft are being built by Northrop Corporation under Dr. Pfenninger's guidance. If an air-inhaling system is also installed in the body of the plane, then its range might be doubled.

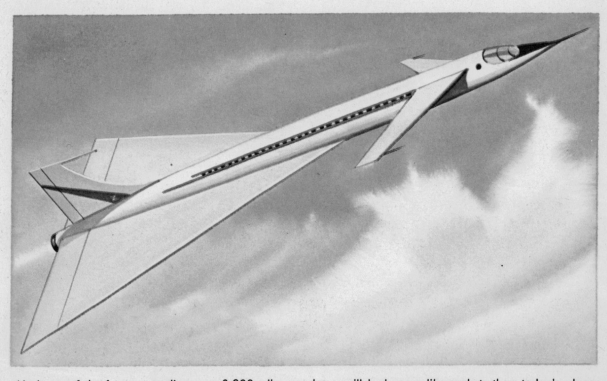

Airplanes of the future, speeding over 2,000 miles per hour, will look more like rockets than today's planes.

RECENT AVIATION HISTORY

Captain Joseph W. Kittinger, Jr., a thirty-one-year-old United States Air Force officer, soared nearly 103,000 feet above the New Mexico desert in an open-gondola balloon on August 16, 1960. He exceeded the old record set by Lieutenant Colonel David G. Simons, using a closed-gondola balloon, by some 500 feet.

After reaching the record height, Kittinger plunged toward the earth. He set a new world's record for free fall (jumping with a parachute closed). He plunged some 17 miles in 4 minutes and 38 seconds. Upon reaching about 17,500 feet, he opened his parachute and descended the remainder of his trip in 8 minutes and 30 seconds.

A new height-record for a balloon was set May 4, 1961 by Navy Commanders Malcolm Ross and Victor Prather. Their helium-filled balloon, with an aluminum-framed gondola, soared to 113,000 feet. Prather was killed during the helicopter rescue.

* * *

In 1959, the experimental military plane, the X-15, made its first free flight. At that time it reached an air speed of about 1,300 miles per hour — and exceeded an altitude of 50,000 feet.

* * *

During the spring of 1961, the X-15 set new records for experimental aircraft. It reached an altitude of 169,600 feet, more than 32 miles above the earth.

* * *

On April 21, 1961, Major Robert M. White of the Air Force set a new world speed record of 3,140 miles per hour in an X-15 rocket plane. The plane was released from a B-52 and achieved the record speed at an altitude of 80,000 feet above the earth.

* * *

In December, 1959, Major Joseph W. Rogers set the world's speed record for conventional jet aircraft for a straightaway course of 1,525 miles per hour. Within a year, on October 4, 1960, Commander John F. Davis of the United States Navy, flying a McDonnell F4H-1 *Phantom II* fighter, set the new world's speed record for a circular course, reaching 1,390.21 miles per hour.

* * *

In 1958, the first commercial jetliner, the Boeing 707, took to the air flying passengers for the airlines. Within the year, in 1959, the airlines also started using the Douglas DC-8. Both jetliners have cruising speeds of about 615 miles per hour and have a normal range of 1,750 miles with full pay-load.

* * *

Jetliners have set many new world speed records. One of the most outstanding has been a United Air Lines DC-8, which flew from Denver to New York City in 3 hours and 31 minutes, at an average air speed of 570 miles per hour.

* * *

Since the days of Daedalus, man has sought to fly with his "own wings." So far, the nearest man has come to this dream has been the one-man helicopter. The Gyrodyne YRON-1 *Rotorcycle* is now in full production for both the United States Navy and the Marine Corps. This small helicopter carries one man easily and can carry heavy loads in addition. It is now being used for map plotting and military observation, and will be used for anti-submarine missions by the United States Navy.

KITTINGER BALLOON

BELL X-15

McDONNELL F4H-1

BOEING 707

DOUGLAS DC-8

GYRODYNE ROTORCYCLE

Rockets, Missiles and Satellites

How were rockets first used? Some historians believe that the Chinese used rockets, similar to our large firecrackers, at about the same time that the ancient Egyptians were building the Great Pyramids. They attached the rockets to arrows to make them fly farther. We do know that in A.D. 1232, during the Mongolian siege of the city of Kaifêng, the Chinese used *fei-i-ho-chien* (sticks of flying fire) to defend themselves. In fourteenth-century Europe, military rockets were used to set fire to cities and terrorize the enemy.

One of the most famous early uses of military rockets was at the Battle of Fort McHenry during the War of 1812. The British launched rockets from boats in conjunction with artillery fire. During the rocket attack, Francis Scott Key, writing the words to the "Star-Spangled Banner," described the red glare of the rockets. Some forty years later, military rockets began to disappear as weapons, because artillery cannons became more efficient.

The first man to attempt to fly a rocket ship•was a Chinese mandarin, Wanhu. About A.D. 1500, he had a bamboo chair "rocket ship" to which forty-seven of the largest rockets available were attached. He sat in the chair and held a large kite in each hand. The kites were to help him glide gently back to earth. At a signal, his assistants ignited the rockets. It is reported that there was a great roar, a blast of flame and smoke — and Wanhu and his ship disappeared. It is unlikely that he flew into space.

Who were the rocket pioneers? Although rockets disappeared as military weapons shortly after the Mexican War in 1847, they continued to be used for signaling at sea during distress, as flares to light battlefields and as fireworks. But the dream of space continued.

An American physicist, Dr. Robert Goddard, began to experiment with rockets in 1908. In 1919, when he published his first report, he revolutionized rocket theory. Up to that time, scientists believed that a rocket flew because its explosion pushed against the air. Dr. Goddard noted that rockets could fly even in "thin" air similar to that found

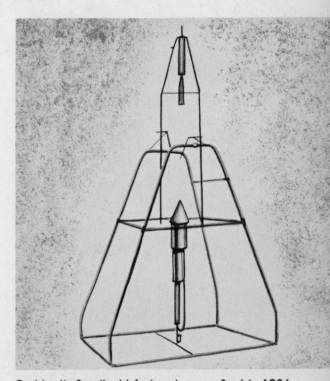

Goddard's first liquid fuel rocket was fired in 1926.

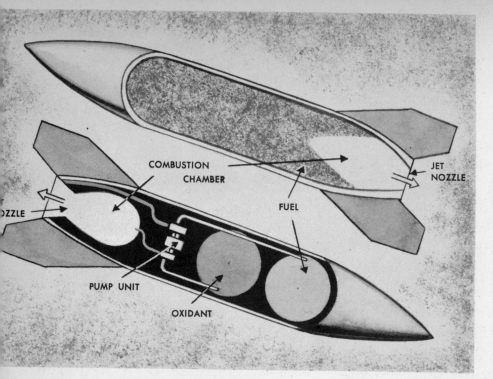

COMBUSTION CHAMBER

JET NOZZLE

FUEL

NOZZLE

PUMP UNIT

OXIDANT

The solid fuel rocket (top) is used for short-range guided missiles and as assisting devices for quick take-off of conventional and jet aircraft. The liquid fuel rocket (below) is used for long-range flights and when high speeds are needed, as in launching satellites.

thousands of feet above the earth. He believed that rockets could be flown to the moon.

Although people ridiculed him and his work, Dr. Goddard continued to experiment. In 1926, he tested the first liquid fuel rocket. It traveled at 60 miles per hour and reached 184 feet in the air. His report and work inspired others in the field of rocketry. In 1929, in Germany, a rocket-propelled glider carried a man in flight.

In 1935, Dr. Goddard launched a gyroscope-controlled rocket. It rose almost 8,000 feet into the air and attained a speed of almost 700 miles per hour. About the same time, a group of Germans interested in rockets formed the *Verein für Raumschiffahrt*, the Rocket Society. One of its members was Count Wernher von Braun who, during World War II, directed rocket research at the German Research Facility at Peenemunde. After the war, von Braun came to the United States and has played a vital role in its rocket program.

What makes a rocket fly? The basic rocket engine is the simplest of all power units for flight. It contains a combustion chamber and an exhaust nozzle. It needs no moving parts. The explosion of the propellent (explosive charge or fuel) escaping from the exhaust creates the forward thrust.

There are many different types of rockets, but they are classified into two groups — solid propellent and liquid propellent. The first group, solid propellents, are somewhat like the large firecrackers used on the Fourth of July. These rockets are powered by an explosive in powder or solid form. The final stage of the rocket that launched the first U. S. *Explorer Satellite* was a solid propellent rocket.

The liquid propellent rockets have more complex power units. It is necessary to have tanks within the rockets to hold the liquid and often pumps to control the flow of the liquid to the combustion chamber. The most commonly used liquid fuel is alcohol and liquid oxygen, or *lox,* as it is often called. The lox, when pumped into a rocket just before blast-off, is extremely cold. Its temperature is −305°F.

Rockets differ from jets in that they are not airbreathing. Because the rockets carry their own oxygen to aid combustion, they can work even in a vacuum, where there is no air. There is no limit to the height they can reach.

What is a guided missile? Any unmanned rocket or ship, whose flight path can be altered while it is still in flight, is known as a guided missile. The first attempt at guided missiles was made by the Germans during World War II. They used V-1 rockets, actually pulsejet engines with explosives, to bombard London. These missiles flew at 360 miles per hour and had a range of about 125 miles. The German V-2 rockets were larger and more powerful. Their range was about 200 miles and they reached speeds of 3,000 miles per hour.

One system of classifying guided missiles is based on (a) where they are fired, and (b) the location of their target. For example, *surface-to-surface* missiles are fired from the ground to hit a target on the ground. Examples of surface-to-surface missiles are the Air Force *Atlas* and *Titan.* Both have a range of 8,000 to 8,500 miles and travel at a speed of over Mach 20 — twenty times the speed of sound. The Navy's *Polaris* is a surface-to-surface missile that can be fired from under water.

Surface-to-air missiles include the Navy's *Talos* and the Army's *Hercules,*

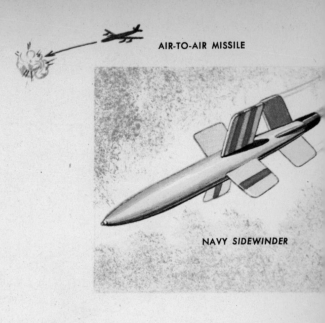

AIR-TO-AIR MISSILE

NAVY *SIDEWINDER*

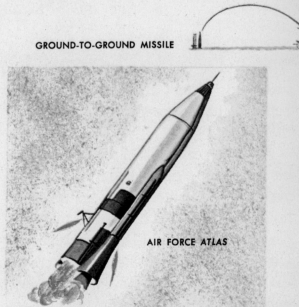

GROUND-TO-GROUND MISSILE

AIR FORCE *ATLAS*

which travel at speeds of over Mach 3 and Mach 4. The Navy's *Sidewinder,* which exceeds a Mach 2.5 speed, is an *air-to-air* missile, while the Army's *Rascal* is an *air-to-surface* missile.

How do they guide missiles? Guided missiles are controlled in flight by radio, radar and electronic computers. When one radar beam picks up the target, it feeds the information about height, direction and speed to a computer. The electronic computer makes all the calculations

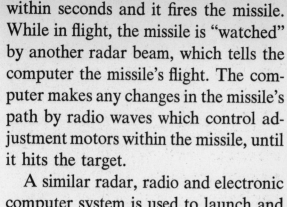

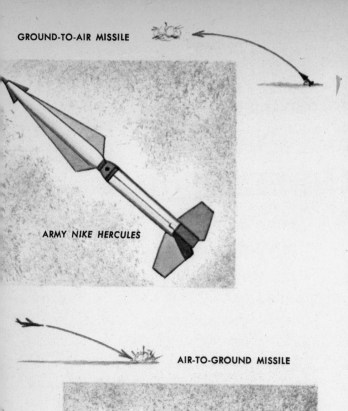

ARMY *NIKE HERCULES*

AIR-TO-GROUND MISSILE

ARMY *RASCAL*

within seconds and it fires the missile. While in flight, the missile is "watched" by another radar beam, which tells the computer the missile's flight. The computer makes any changes in the missile's path by radio waves which control adjustment motors within the missile, until it hits the target.

A similar radar, radio and electronic computer system is used to launch and guide rockets as they go off into space. Large radar and radio telescope units "follow" the rocket as it plunges into space. If the rocket veers off course, these watchers inform the computer and it radios the rocket, making the necessary changes to correct its course.

You know that if you throw a ball into the air, it will fall back to earth. This "pull" of the earth is called *gravity*. There is a rule which governs moving bodies —a moving body will continue to travel in a straight line unless acted on by another force.

Why does a satellite stay up in the sky?

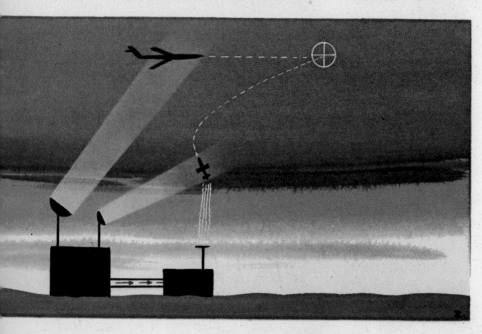

The main radar scanner (left) picks up approaching aircraft. A computer works out the plane's speed, path, height, weather conditions and other factors. The ground missile is automatically made ready and fired by the computer. A smaller radar guides the missile through the air until it reaches the enemy target.

If the ball were shot up like a rocket, traveling at about 18,000 miles per hour, to a height of 300 miles, it would be affected by two forces. One is the force of gravity that would pull it back to earth, and the other is the force that would tend to keep it moving in a straight line. At this speed and at this height, these two forces would be about equal. As a result, the ball would continue to spin around the earth. That is just what the satellite does.

The speed needed to overcome the earth's gravitational pull is called the *escape velocity*. You can compare this with rolling a toy automobile up a small hill. If the car is not pushed fast enough, it will slow up as it goes up the hill, stop for an instant and then roll back down the hill. If it is pushed fast enough, it will roll over the top of the hill and continue rolling. That escape velocity from the earth is about 25,000 miles per hour. Thus, for a satellite to remain in orbit,

it must attain a speed of at least 18,000 miles per hour. If it is to escape the earth's gravitational pull in order to go into outer space, it must be traveling at over 25,000 miles per hour.

Satellites have been used to discover the mysteries of the

What do satellites see and *tell*? upper atmosphere and interplanetary space. Satellites with various shapes have been used, including spheres, cones, cylinders, spheres with paddles and even a giant balloon. Each of the satellites has been packed with scientific instruments, and their readings have been sent back to earth by radio. We have even mounted photographic and television cameras in satellites.

While the initial satellites tested our ability to put a satellite into orbit and to track it, the later ones went into space on specific probes. *Explorer I* studied the cosmic rays, or van Allen radiation belt, around the earth. *Vanguard I* measured the density of the air in our upper atmosphere and space.

The Russian *Lunik* satellites were moon "explorers." *Lunik I* studied the atmosphere around the moon, *Lunik II*

Rockets carry satellite into the air so it can take off under its own power. The satellite is kept in orbit as the centrifugal force is balanced by the gravitational pull of the earth.

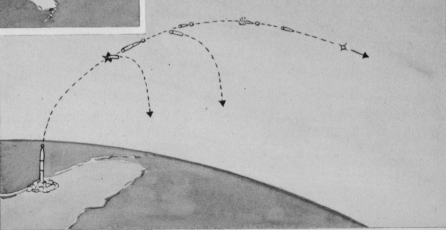

46

landed on the moon, and *Lunik III* photographed the "dark side" of the moon, the side which no man had ever seen before.

The American *Tiros I*, equipped with television cameras and transmitters, sent back TV pictures of the cloud covers over the earth. *Explorer XII* tested our ability to recover a capsule returned to earth from the satellite. *Echo I* was put into orbit to aid long-range voice communications by bouncing radio-wave telephone messages off its massive surface.

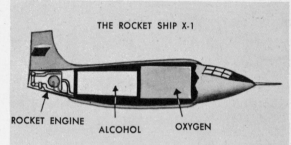

THE ROCKET SHIP X-1

ROCKET ENGINE   ALCOHOL   OXYGEN

Steppingstones Into Space

On October 14, 1947, there were two

Has man flown in a rocket?

planes some six miles up in the sky over California. One was a four-engine B-29 and the other, painted bright orange, was fastened to the B-29's underside. Suddenly, the orange plane, like a stone fired from a slingshot, soared upward and exceeded Mach 1, the speed of sound. That plane was the X-1, a rocket ship piloted by Captain Charles E. Yeager.

The X-1 was shaped like a .50-caliber bullet. It was 31 feet long and its wingspan was 28 feet. It was powered by a rocket engine using liquid oxygen and alcohol as fuel.

Some six years later, Yeager flew the X-1A. He zoomed more than 90,000 feet into the air, traveling at a speed of 1,650 miles per hour. These early rocket ships were followed by others, including the X-3, the *Flying Stiletto,* and the X-5, the *Flying Guppy.*

The X-15, an outstanding rocket ship, was developed for speeds of up to 4,000 miles per hour and a flight ceiling of 100 miles. This 50-foot ship has a 22-foot wingspan and is launched in the air from a giant B-52 at 40,000 to 50,000 feet. Its rocket engine is designed to fire for only 90 seconds. After that the rocket glides back to earth. Many consider the X-15 the first true manned rocket ship.

On October 11, 1961, Major Robert M. White set an altitude record in the X-15 by flying it more than 41 miles above the earth. On November 9, 1961, in a maximum effort, he set a speed record of 4,070 miles per hour.

The X-15 is the forerunner of the first real space rocket, the Boeing *Dyna-Soar.* This manned rocket is designed for speeds of up to Mach 25 — twenty-five times the speed of sound, or 17,000 miles per hour. It is designed so that it can escape the earth's atmosphere.

On April 27, 1959, seven astronauts (AS-tro-nauts) — three from the Air Force, three from the Navy and one from the Marine Corps — were selected for *Project Mercury*. This project has three objectives: (1) to study man's ability to travel in space; (2) to place a manned satellite in orbit around the earth; and (3) to return the pilot safely to earth.

What is Project Mercury?

A special capsule has been built to hold the pilot. This cone-shaped capsule, 7 feet in diameter at its base and 10 feet long, will be the satellite which is eventually placed in orbit by a rocket. Within the capsule, the pilot will be strapped to a couchlike frame to support him against the intense pressures during take-off and landing. The cone-capsule will go into orbit at 100 to 150 miles above the earth. At re-entry time, retro-rockets, attached to the capsule, will be fired. This will slow the capsule and make it return to earth. The capsule has a special re-entry shield to protect the pilot from the intense heat that will be created when the capsule re-enters the earth's atmosphere.

On April 12, 1961, the Soviet Union launched the first manned satellite to orbit the earth. The 5-ton space vehicle

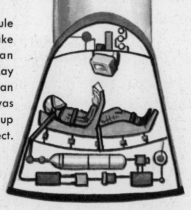

The Mercury capsule was designed to take the first American into space. On May 5, 1961, Com. Alan B. Shepard Jr. was fired 115 miles up in the U. S. project.

z.

Space craft will one day land on the earth's moon.

reached a 188-mile height and, traveling at a speed exceeding 17,000 miles per hour, circled the earth in 89.1 minutes. The Russian pilot, Major Yuri Gagarin, was returned to earth alive.

On May 5, 1961, the United States launched its first manned satellite. It was also the world's first space flight controlled by a pilot — Navy Commander Alan B. Shepard Jr. The 2,000-pound Mercury capsule, named *Freedom 7,* was fired by a Redstone rocket. The craft, traveling at a speed of 4,500 miles per hour, reached an altitude of 115 miles during the 15-minute trip.

Man no longer needs to envy the bird. Not only can he fly faster and farther than any bird, but he can also fly in the air-thin atmosphere.

What about the future?

Man has always been curious about space — the moon, planets, other worlds. As far back as A.D. 160, the Greek philosopher, Lucian of Samosata, wrote a tale about a trip to the moon. Today, man is at the threshold of space, ready to turn fictional moon journeys into reality.